This book belongs to:

____

Inspired by a special Kindergarten Class

Cookies in Heaven, New Covenant Grace Publications, by Joyce Carlin

ISBN 9798608470356

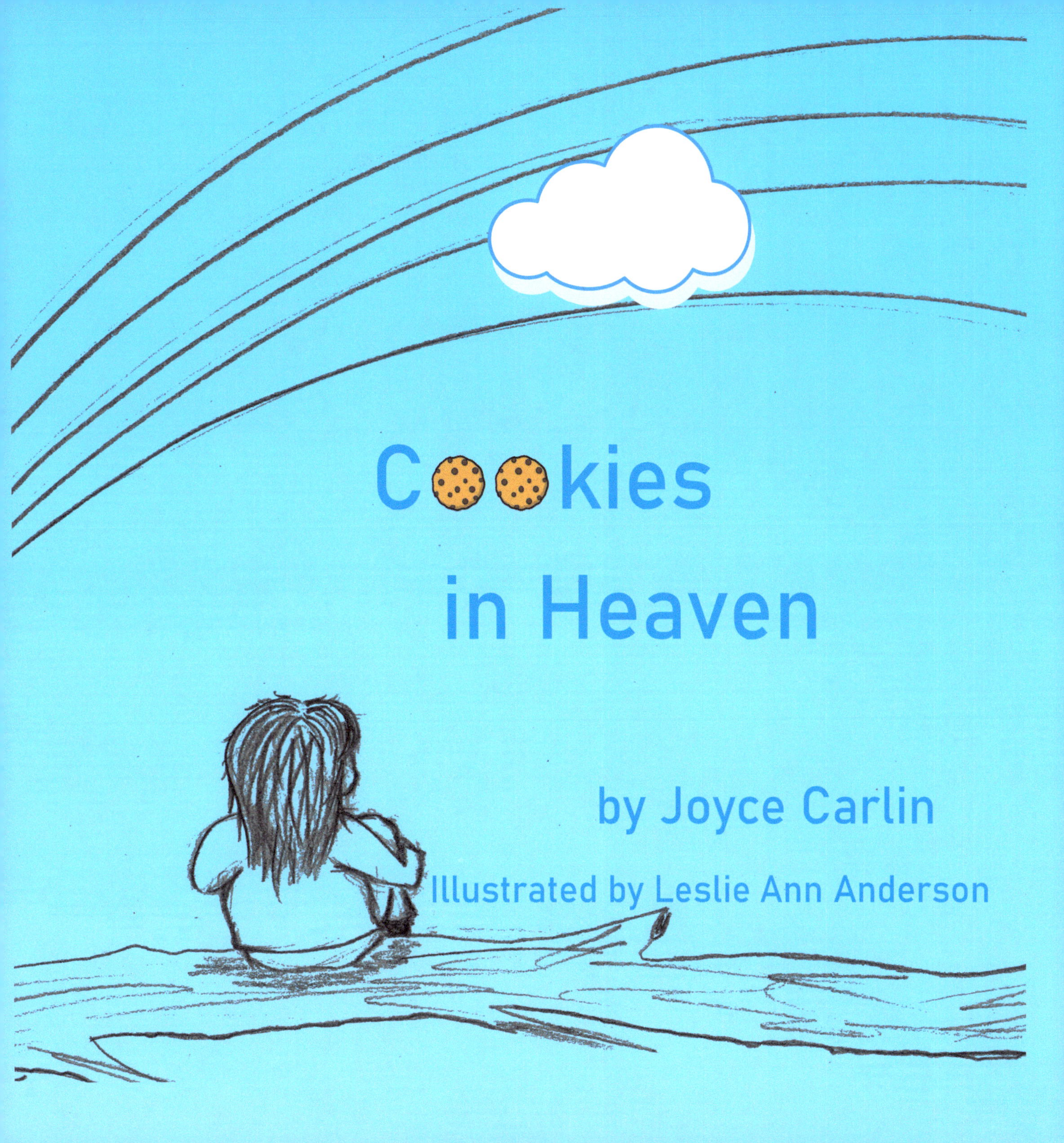

Cookies
in Heaven
by Joyce Carlin
Illustrated by Leslie Ann Anderson

There once was
a special teacher.

She was silly, and kind, and smart,
and pretty.

I thought all these things about her and
so they were true...

In the beginning, I did not know
how wonderful my teacher was.

But, I found out right away.

LEARNING
IS
FUN

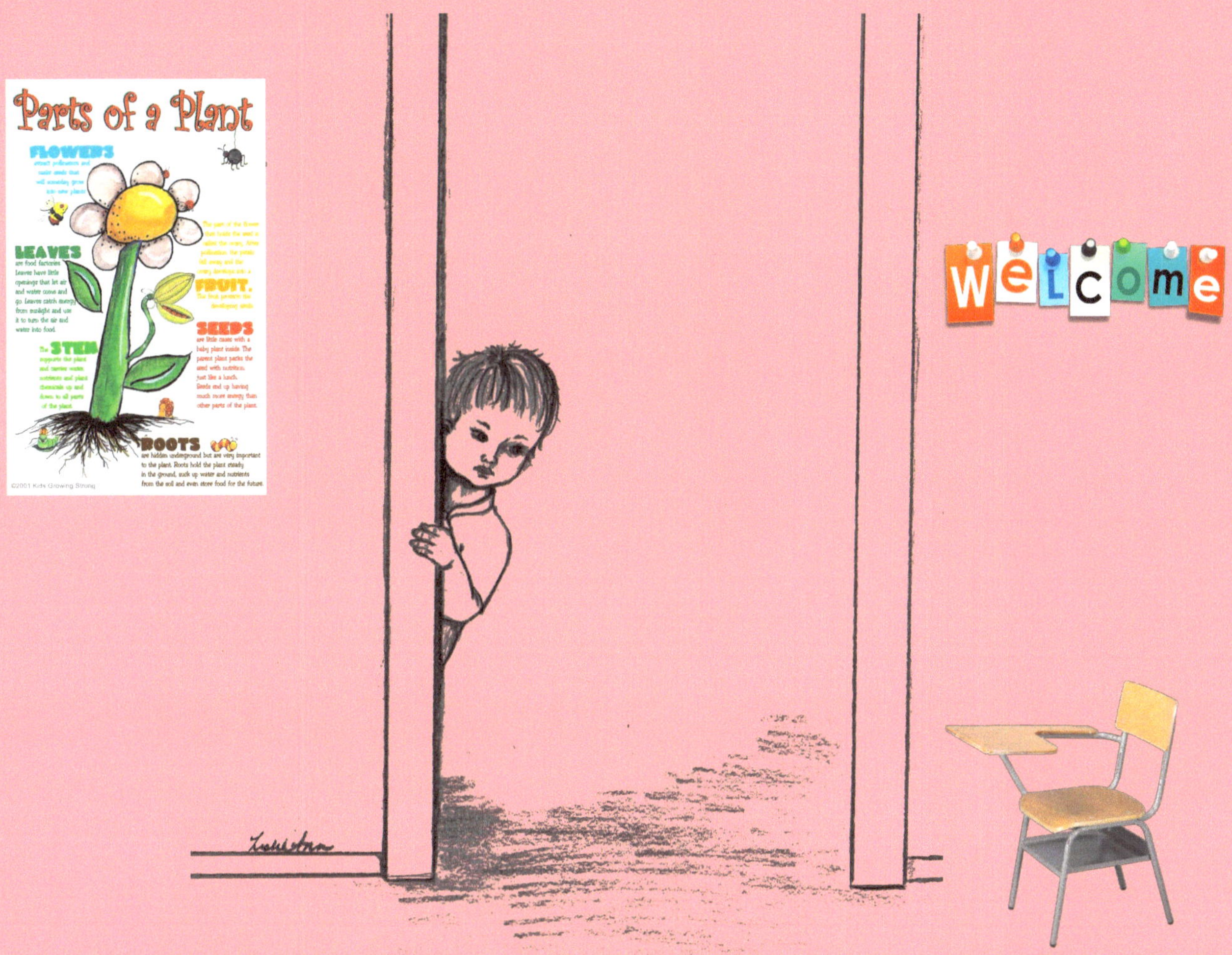

She took my hand for the very first time and

whispered that everything would be okay

because she was going to stay with me the

And every day, my teacher had new ideas
and things to see.

I would always laugh when she made funny
faces in class.

And, I would smile when she said, "Well done!"
And then,

she would smile too.

ABCDEFGHIJKLMN
OPQRSTUVWXYZ

1-2-3-4-5-6-7-8-9-10-11

12-13-14-15-16-17-18-19

20... ⟶ 100!

Once, she taught me to read
my alphabet and to count all the way
to one hundred!

The older I grew, the more she taught me.

2+2=4, and

caterpillars become

butterflies!

Now I know that shapes have names and
that hair grows back after you
cut it.

My teacher could fix almost anything with tape
or glue. I liked that because things always seem
to tear...

or...

break.

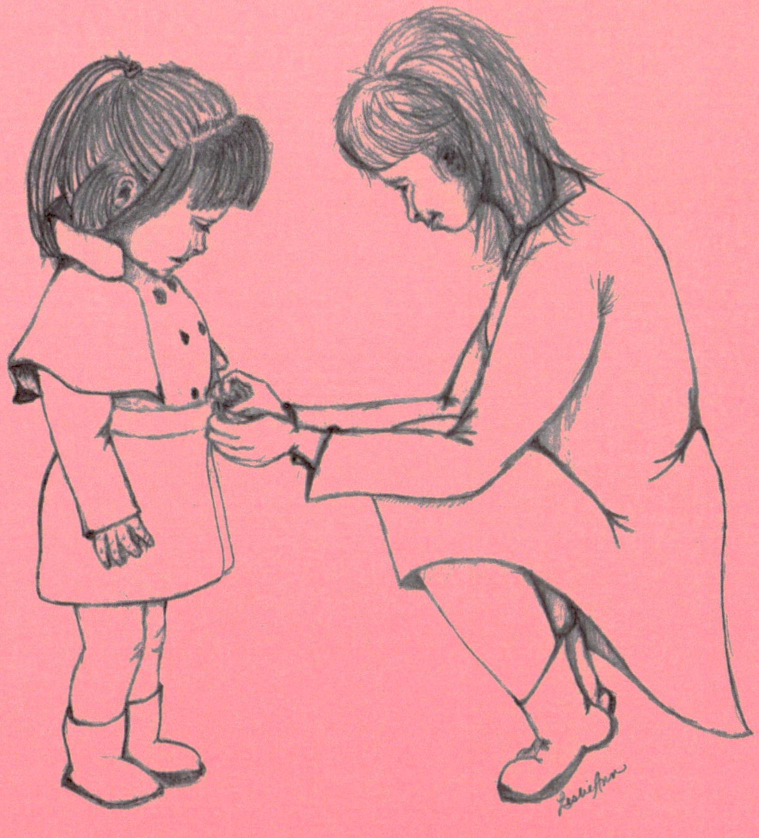

She would tell me to, "Be careful."

And, I would try again.

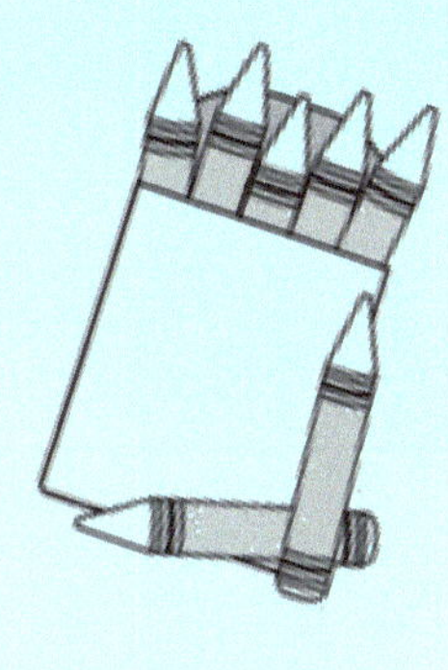

Not every teacher knows when you need a
hug or a black crayon. These were things my
special teacher always knew.

She

would

even

let

us...

stick out our tongues on "Th"ursday and
pretend to hide her eyes. That was
so-o-o-o funny!

One day, my teacher taught us about Jesus and how He came to gather His special sheep. She said Jesus died on a cross to make sure no one would be left on the playground or anywhere else. That's what shepherds do.

I think that special teachers are like that too.

After that, I would imagine that I

was one of those sheep.

Then, one day, she told us about Heaven. She said we would all go there one day. I did not like it when she told us that, probably,

she

would go

there...

...without us. My eyes watered a lot and my chest hurt.

And then, my teacher said something wonderful. She said that when she got to Heaven, she would straightaway start baking cookies for when we came to Heaven.

She promised to have a great, big party when
we got there. That sounded awesome!
But, mostly, it sounded

Delicious!

I have had many cookies

since

those school days.

I have even had a few more teachers.

But, none of my teachers were like her. Most of them do not even know about Jesus or cookies.

It is really just our secret about the cookies...

But, the part about Jesus stays in my heart
and so I know it is true.

Now if I close my eyes very tightly, I can see
my teacher's face.
And if I think about it for very long, I am sure
that I smell cookies baking.

After all...

...my teacher promised us cookies

in Heaven and so, I know...

...that it is true.